Baby on Board
How Animals Carry Their Young

By Marianne Berkes
Illustrated by Cathy Morrison

Dawn Publications

For Missy, the best daughter a mother could have. Love you forever. —MB

To my grandson, Konnor, the cutest baby ever! —CM

Copyright © 2017 Marianne Berkes
Illustrations copyright © 2017 Cathy Morrison

All rights reserved. No part of this book may be reproduced or transmitted to any form or by any means, electronic or mechanical, including photocopying, recording, or by any information and retrieval system, without written permission from the publisher.

Library of Congress Cataloging-in-Publication Data

Names: Berkes, Marianne Collins. | Morrison, Cathy, illustrator.
Title: Baby on board : how animals carry their young / by Marianne Berkes ;
 illustrated by Cathy Morrison. First edition Other titles: How animals carry their young
Description: Nevada City, CA : Dawn Publications, [2017] | Audience: Age 3-7.
Identifiers: LCCN 2016024976| ISBN 9781584695929 (hard)
 | ISBN 9781584695936 (pbk.)
Subjects: LCSH: Parental behavior in animals--Juvenile literature.
 | Animals--Infancy--Juvenile literature.
Classification: LCC QL762 .B47 2017 | DDC 591.56/3--dc23
 LC record available at https://lccn.loc.gov/2016024976

Book design and computer production by Patty Arnold,
Menagerie Design & Publishing

Manufactured by Regent Publishing Services, Hong Kong
Printed December, 2016, in ShenZhen, Guangdong, China
10 9 8 7 6 5 4 3 2 1
First Edition

DAWN PUBLICATIONS
Road
959
55
nature@dawn   om

When you were a baby, someone carried you.
Have you ever wondered what animal parents do?

There are no baby backpacks,
no wraps or straps or slings,
no seats to buckle kids in,
or many other things.

This mother baby carrier is one that is well-known.
Her joey lives inside her pouch until he's nearly grown.

Kangaroo

At birth, the baby, called a joey, is guided safely
into a pouch where it is protected while it nurses.

This mom is like a living raft as she transports her pup.
She hunts for food for both of them and never will give up.

Sea Otter

Before she goes out to hunt for food, a mother sea otter wraps her baby in long strands of kelp seaweed to keep her pup from drifting away.

Baby clings on mama's hair. They slowly move with ease.
They sleep while hanging upside down from branches
    in the trees.

Sloth

As soon as it is born, the baby sloth clutches its mother's hairy belly with its long claws and stays really close for almost a year.

This animal hauls her babies from one place to another.
The joeys have it easy as they all ride on their mother.

Opossum

The opossum mother spends a lot of time
and energy carrying her litter of joeys from
one home to another.

They paddle very slowly as they swim along the coast.
But nestled under mama's fin, this baby likes it most.

Manatee

A baby manatee, called a calf, can swim within minutes after birth. But it remains close to its mother, nursing behind the mother's flipper.

This mother carries baby right upon her chest.
At evening she will place it in a "sleeping" nest.

Chimpanzee

A mother chimp carries her baby in the crook of her arm close to her chest during the day. Each night she prepares a new sleeping nest for her baby.

This baby's downy feathers hold body heat inside.
It climbs on top of papa's back, and they go for a ride.

Common Loon

Both common loon parents care for their young,
usually one or two. Carrying them on their backs
keeps chicks safe from fish and turtle predators.

When babies call their mother, there is no time to pause.
She carries them to safety, gripped in her powerful jaws.

Alligator

Alligator hatchlings vocalize, which attracts their mother back to the nest. She gently lifts them out, a few at a time, and carries them to the water for safety.

This baby carrier mother aggressively keeps track,
As hundreds of her spiderlings climb right
onto her back.

Wolf Spider

Spiderlings crowd onto their mother's back as soon as they are
hatched. Most people do not recognize them as baby spiders
until they move out from the tightly packed group.

The mother lays a single egg.
Then she goes out to sea.
The father warms it on his feet.
How can this really be?

Emperor Penguin

In the bitter cold of Antarctica, the female emperor penguin lays an egg.
Then the male keeps it warm by balancing it on his feet under
a flap of skin until the chick hatches.

Blending in with mama's fur, you hardly see this pup.
It rides upon her hairy back while
she digs insects up.

Anteater

Mama anteater collects ants and termites with her long sticky tongue. The pattern on her pup's fur helps camouflage it from predators.

The female hides her little cubs before she hunts for prey.
When she comes back, she picks them up if they have gone astray.

Lion

The mother, called a lioness, hides her young cubs in dense bushes
for safety before going out to hunt for prey.

Tucked in pouches, gripped in teeth,
Propped on backs, or underneath,
This is what some animals do.
How did someone carry you?

Match Game:

Match the name of the animal to the description of how the parent carries its baby.

1. Kangaroo
A. I prepare a new sleeping nest for my baby every night.

2. Sea Otter
B. We paddle together in the warm water along the coast.

3. Sloth
C. My chick climbs on my back for safety and to keep warm.

4. Opossum
D. My baby clings onto my hair as we move very slowly.

5. Manatee
E. I wrap my pup in kelp seaweed before I hunt for food.

6. Chimpanzee
F. When my eggs hatch, hundreds of babies climb on my back.

7. Common Loon
G. I carry my litter of joeys on my back going from place to place.

8. Alligator
H. I warm the egg that my mate has laid on my feet.

9. Wolf Spider
I. When I hunt for prey, I hide my cubs in dense bushes for safety.

10. Emperor Penguin
J. My pup blends in with my fur while I dig up insects.

11. Anteater
K. My joey is safely tucked in my pouch when I hop.

12. Lion
L. I hurry back to the nest when my hatchlings vocalize.

Answers: 1 - K, 2 - E, 3 - D, 4 - G, 5 - B, 6 - A, 7 - C, 8 - L, 9 - F, 10 - H, 11 - J, 12 - I.

A Read Aloud Suggestion:

Before showing children the illustrations, read the verse aloud and have them guess what animal is being described. Then show them the illustration and read the additional information on each page. You may also share the fun facts below.

Kangaroos live in Australia and Tasmania. They are the largest animals in the world that mainly get around by hopping. There are four distinct species—the Eastern Gray is shown in this book.

Sea Otters have thick fur to keep them warm in the cold water of the Pacific Ocean. They eat shellfish, often breaking open shells by smashing them against a rock that they carry with them.

Three-toed Sloths live in the rainforests of Central and South America. They spend most of their time hanging in treetops, sleeping 18 hours a day. They get all their food from the trees—leaves, shoots, and fruit.

Opossums nurse their young in a pouch, which means that they are marsupials like kangaroos. They're comfortable living around people, but we don't usually see them because they're nocturnal.

West Indian Manatees are sometimes called sea cows. They are slow-moving mammals found in warm, shallow rivers and along coastal areas from the eastern U.S. to South America.

Chimpanzees live in African rainforests, woodlands, and grasslands. Chimps use tools, including twigs to fish for termites, rocks to smash nuts, and leaves to soak up water like sponges.

Common Loons live on lakes and along the coasts of North America. Their red eyes help them see underwater as they dive down deep to catch fish.

American Alligators live in the slow-moving water of swamps, marshes, and lakes in the southeastern United States. Their mouths hold about 80 teeth, and their jaws are strong enough to crack a turtle shell.

Wolf Spiders are often found in gardens and near homes. They don't make a web, but stalk their prey on the ground. They are fast runners and sometimes hide in tunnels to ambush crickets and other insects.

Emperor Penguins "fly" through the water with wings like paddles. Their thick feathers keep them warm in the icy water of the coldest place on Earth—Antarctica. They're the deepest diving bird, catching fish to eat.

Giant Anteaters live in Central and South America. They don't have any teeth, but they have very long, sticky tongues. They lap up as many as 30,000 ants in a day.

African Lions live on the savanna in a family group called a pride. The females are the pride's primary hunters. They often work together to catch zebras and other large animals.

Language Arts:

Listening Skills and Vocabulary Development —After reading the book aloud, ask children the following questions. Refer to the rhyming text and illustrations to confirm the answers. Ask children to define the italicized words in context and then read the definitions.

☸ Which baby is *camouflaged* by the pattern on its fur? (Anteater) *Camouflage*: colors or shapes that protect an animal from attack by making it difficult to see them.

☸ Which baby is wrapped in *strands* of seaweed? (Sea Otter) *Strands*: something that looks like a long rope.

☸ Which animal parent in the book has a *litter*? (Opossum) *Litter*: a group of babies all born at the same time.

☸ Which baby animal is protected from fish and turtle *predators*? (Common Loon) *Predator*: an animal that lives by killing and eating other animals.

- Which animal hides her babies before she goes out to hunt for *prey?* (Lioness) *Prey:* an animal that is hunted or killed by another animal for food.

- Which animal parent *aggressively* protects her eggs? (Wolf Spider) *Aggressive:* acting forcefully and being ready to attack.

- Which *hatchlings vocalize* to get their mother's attention? (Alligator) *Hatchling:* an animal that has just hatched out of its shell. *Vocalize:* to make a sound.

- Whose babies have gone *astray?* (Lioness) *Astray:* away from what is desirable.

- Which baby animal *clutches* onto its mother's hairy belly? (Sloth) *Clutch:* to hold on tightly.

Math: How Many? More or Less?

- How many baby animals are mammals? Birds? Reptiles? Arachnids?

- How many animals are nocturnal (active at night)? How many are diurnal (active during the day)?

- How many animals are carnivores? Herbivores? Omnivores?

- Who has more babies—a wolf spider or an opossum? An opossum or a lioness?

- Who has the least number of babies—an alligator or a kangaroo? A lioness or a sea otter?

Science: Same/Different—Choose two animals and create a Venn diagram to show how they are the same and different from each other. For example, compare and contrast a kangaroo mother and an opossum mother, a loon chick and a penguin chick, or a sea otter and a manatee.

Engineering: How to Carry a Baby—Have each child bring in a stuffed animal as "their baby" and ask them to solve the following problem: they have to hold their baby close to their body wherever they go. Provide materials, such as ribbons, string, tape, belts, and scissors. When finished, have children "wear" their baby and explain their design.

Movement: Who Am I?—Have one child come into the center of a circle to act out how an animal parent moves with its baby, while other children guess the name of the animal. For example, a kangaroo hops with a baby in its pouch and an anteater sticks out its tongue while carrying a baby on its back.

Resources

Live Science—livescience.com/animals

Sea World—www.seaworld.org/animal-info

World Animal Foundation—www.worldanimalfoundation.net

Amazing Moms: Love and Lessons from the Animal Kingdom, Rachel Buchholz, National Geographic

Mother's Love: Inspiring True Stories from the Animal Kingdom, by Melina Gerosa Bellows, National Geographic

Born in the Wild: Baby Animals and Their Parents, by Lita Judge, Roaring Brook Press

Don't Miss It! There are many useful resources online for most of Dawn's books, including activities and standards-based lesson plans. Scan this code to go directly to activities for this book, or go to www.dawnpub.com and click on "Activities" for this and other books.

Marianne Berkes has spent much of her life as a teacher, children's theater director, and children's librarian. She puts these experiences to good use in over 20 entertaining and educational picture books that make a child's learning relevant. Reading, writing, music, and theater have been a constant in Marianne's life. Her books are also inspired by her love of nature. She hopes to open kids' eyes to the magic found in our natural world. Marianne now writes full time. She is an energetic presenter at schools and literary conferences nationwide. Her web site is www.MarianneBerkes.com.

Cathy Morrison is an award-winning illustrator who lives in Northern Colorado, within view of both the Great Plains and the Rocky Mountains. She began her career in animation and graphic design, but discovered her passion for children's book illustration while raising her two children. She feels we are hardwired to love and protect babies, both human and animals, because they are so irresistibly cute (most especially her grandson!). After several years illustrating with traditional media, she now works digitally, which helps the publisher adapt the art into interactive book apps. This is Cathy's sixth book for Dawn Publications.

More Books Illustrated by Cathy Morrison

The Prairie That Nature Built—Go above, below, and all around this beautiful and exciting habitat.

Pitter and Patter—Take a ride with Pitter and Patter, two water drops, as they flow through the water cycle.

If You Love Honey: Nature's Connections—Honey is a sweet gift from nature—ALL of nature!

Wild Ones: Observing City Critters—Animals are everywhere in the city! Look closely to meet them.

More Books by Marianne Berkes

Over in the Ocean — With unique and outstanding style, this book portrays a vivid community of marine creatures.

Over in the Jungle — As with "Ocean," this book captures a rain forest teeming with remarkable animals.

Over in the Arctic — Another charming counting rhyme introduces creatures of the tundra.

Over in Australia — Australian animals are often unique, many with pouches for the babies. Such fun!

Over in the Forest — Follow the tracks of forest animals, but watch out for the skunk!

Over in a River —Beavers, manatees and so many more animals help teach the geography of 10 great North American rivers.

Over on a Mountain —Twenty cool animals, ten great mountain ranges, and seven continents all in one story!

Over in the Grasslands — Come along on a safari. Kids will love to count and sing about the animals they meet. Lions and rhinos and hippos, oh my!

Over on the Farm — Welcome to the farm, where pigs roll, goats nibble, horses gallop, and turkeys strut. Also illustrated by Cathy Morrison.

Going Around the Sun: Some Planetary Fun — Earth is part of a fascinating "family" of planets. Here's a glimpse of the "neighborhood."

Going Home: The Mystery of Animal Migration — Many animals migrate "home," often over great distances.

Seashells by the Seashore — Kids discover, identify, and count twelve beautiful shells to give Grandma for her birthday.

The Swamp Where Gator Hides — Still as a log, only his watchful eyes can be seen. But when gator moves, watch out!

What's in the Garden? — Good food doesn't begin on a store shelf in a box. It comes from a garden bursting with life!

Dawn Publications is dedicated to inspiring in children a deeper understanding and appreciation for all life on Earth. You can browse through our titles, download resources for teachers, and order at www.dawnpub.com or call 800-545-7475.